NATURAL
REMEDIES
FROM THE
JAPANESE
KITCHEN

New York • **WEATHERHILL** • Tokyo

NATURAL REMEDIES FROM THE JAPANESE KITCHEN

HIROKO FUKUHARA

YASUKO TAKAHATA

First edition, 1998

Published by Weatherhill, Inc.
568 Broadway, Suite 705, New York, New York 10012

Printed in Hong Kong.

Library of Congress Cataloging-in-Publication Data

Fukuhara, Hiroko.
   Natural remedies from the Japanese kitchen / Hiroko Fukuhara,
   Yasuko Takahata.—1st ed.
      p. cm.
Includes index.
ISBN 0–8348–0414–x
1. Diet therapy. 2. Cookery, Japanese. I. Takahata, Yasuko. II. Title.
RM219.F896 1998
615.8' 54' 0952—dc21   98–18624
                                                    CIP

CONTENTS

INTRODUCTION

We all want to live long, healthy lives. Have the sciences of medicine, pharmacology, and nutrition succeeded in banishing illness from our world? The answer, unfortunately, is no. Science has, however, continued to make advances in the understanding of nature's ecosystems, of which we human beings are an integral part. They are within us, without us—they are us. The first step in identifying the factors that create and preserve our health is identifying our part in those ecosystems.

Ecosystems are complicated relationships of energy exchange, of eater and eaten. We are what we eat, and to know how to stay healthy, we need first and foremost to know what we as living organisms are designed to eat. Knowing our ideal, natural diet, a diet in harmony with our natural ecosystem, is the key to health, whether we want to preserve our health or restore it.

The traditional Japanese diet, as we shall see below, is very close to the ideal diet for the human animal. Still, in spite of the best diet, illnesses occur for a variety of reasons, internal and external. The key to Japanese remedies is that they are based on the Japanese kitchen—the belief that food is the best medicine. The remedies in this book are all based on everyday Japanese foods. Some are staple grains, such as brown rice and buckwheat. Beans and bean products—soybeans, tofu, soy sauce, natto, black beans, and red beans—also play a very important role. Green, yellow, and root vegetables such as spinach, pumpkin, carrot, ginger, and lotus root are also key ingredients, as are certain pickled foods, especially pickled plums, and teas.

This book is organized by food. The properties of each food are described briefly, followed by at least one remedy using that food as its main ingredient. Poor diet is a major cause of illness, and the best way to prevent sickness is to eat right all the time. In that spirit, we have also included several recipes for delicious dishes incorporating the featured ingredient in each section. These are Japanese dishes, prepared using Japanese cooking techniques, which are explained in each recipe. As in all Japanese cooking, we have made a special effort to make the dishes as visually attractive as they are tasty, so that you can prepare them not only for yourself and your family but for guests as well. Once you get the feel for the simple preparation methods, feel free to adapt and experiment. As long as you keep the basic ingredients, the recipes will retain their curative benefits.

Following this brief introduction, we have appended a list of illnesses and symptoms to help the reader find the best foods for each ailment. Use it as a quick reference and a more natural pathway to exploring the nearly 100 remedies and recipes from the Japanese kitchen that we have gathered here.

We have written this book based on many years of experience in the laboratory, the classroom, and the kitchen. Based on that experience, we have arrived at deep-seated beliefs about nutrition and health, and we'd like to share them with our readers.

A DIET OF GRAINS AND VEGETABLES

Our bodies are made of the food we eat. Our growth from six or seven pounds at birth to twenty, thirty, or even forty times that at maturity is fueled solely by the food we eat. That's what makes diet such an important part of our lives. From long ago it has been said, "Food is life." The elements in our food determine the makeup of our bodies. In other words, it is what we eat that makes us either strong and healthy or weak and susceptible to illness. Food is also what determines whether, once we fall ill, we recover quickly or slowly, or not at all.

The human species first appeared in the tropical and subtropical zones, regions with plentiful rainfall, warm temperatures, and lush vegetation. Grains, beans, and many varieties of vegetables and fruits grew there. For hundreds of thousands of years, the human race evolved on this diet of foods widely available in the tropical and subtropical regions, and as a result our biological functions are exceptionally well adapted to a diet of grains and vegetables.

Our teeth reflect this adaptation very clearly. We have twenty molars for grinding and chewing grains and beans, eight incisors for biting leafy matter, and only four cuspids, or canine teeth, for tearing meat. This represents a grains and beans to leafy greens to meat ratio of 5 to 2 to 1, or of vegetable matter to meat of 7 to 1. We can see from this that human beings are meant to eat a primarily vegetarian diet.

A look at our digestive enzymes leads to the same conclusion. Our saliva consists almost completely of the enzyme amylases, which digests starch. This amylases increases tremendously in activity after weaning. At the same time, the activity of the enzyme lactase, which metabolizes the milk sugar, lactose, drops suddenly and drastically. In other words, after weaning human beings lose their ability to digest lactose efficiently and suddenly acquire the ability to digest starch very efficiently, as our bodies prepare to switch from a diet of milk to one of grains and vegetables.

As humanity spread north from the tropical and subtropical zones, to regions with long cold winters which limited the availability of grains and vegetables, it was forced to adapt to a diet with increased amounts of meat and dairy products. Europeans and other northern peoples now have more active lactase enzyme as adults than do peoples of warmer climes.

Our intestines also tell us about our natural diet. They are of medium length, ranging between the intestines of herbivores and carnivores. Interestingly, the intestines of Europeans and other northern peoples forced to eat meat and dairy products for thousands of years are somewhat shorter than most Asian peoples, who have remained on a primarily vegetarian diet. This change in the length of the intestine is a special adaptation, because shorter intestines allow the harmful and noxious digestive byproducts of meat to be evacuated from the system as quickly as possible.

Though there are such differences between peoples of temperate and tropical regions, all human beings are basically built to subsist mostly on grains and vegetables, and excessive consumption of meat is inevitably harmful to all of us. The sharp increases in cancer, heart disease, and obesity that have accompanied the Westernization of diet around the world are a warning that we are not eating the diet to which our species is best adapted.

Recent research on human diet during the Old Stone Age as well as studies of surviving hunting and gathering peoples show that grains, nuts, vegetables, roots and tubers, and fruit made up the main portion of their diet. By no coincidence, the ratio of vegetable to animal matter in both diets has been shown to be about 7 to 1—-exactly what our teeth tell us it should be.

OUR FOOD IS KILLING US

In today's world, we find ourselves surrounded on all sides by an enormous variety and amount of meat products and processed foods. They are spread out before us like a banquet wherever we look, at the supermarket, the convenience store, the diner, the delicatessen, and the fast-food restaurant. They have invaded our homes and occupy our dinner tables.

We human beings, designed to digest starch, are not only biologically incapable of processing the large amounts of meat and processed foods we consume today, they actually stress and harm our system. It is clear that years and generations of this constitutionally unsuitable diet have produced, in the populations of the developed nations, epidemic levels of various life-threatening diseases, such as obesity, arteriosclerosis, heart disease, cancer, diabetes, allergies, and even mental illness. Yet when we fall ill and we look for the cause of the illness, very few indeed look to the most important part of their daily lives: diet. Almost none realize that most illnesses are caused by the harm wreaked on our biological systems and processes by an unsuitable diet. The vast majority decide that their illness is caused by something outside themselves, and that it can be cured by some drug or medicine. The sad fact is that chronic illness cannot be cured by drugs. Drugs, in most cases, are not deigned to cure a chronic disease, only alleviate its symptoms. Often they worsen the patient's general condition and, with their attendant side effects, carry the risk of fostering the emergence of even worse illnesses.

The United States, whose population is threatened by a sudden and dramatic rise in such chronic conditions as cancer and heart disease, has conducted global research on the relationship between diet and chronic illness. The results of the McGovern Report were announced in 1977, with recommendations for an immediate change in the American diet. What were those recommendations? An increase in whole grains and a reduction in sugar and meat.

The United States government has now decided to try to improve the American diet by recommending a sharp increase in the amount of whole grains, making them the main part of the diet. In fact, epidemiologic studies have shown that until recently, most of the world's peoples consumed a diet based heavily on whole grains, and people who adhered to such a diet were not commonly afflicted with such chronic illnesses as cancer and heart disease. In addition, whole grains are the main component of the diets of all regions of the world with the longest life expectancies.

The three major grains cultivated around the globe are wheat, rice, and corn. Rice is nutrionally superior to both wheat and corn, for a variety of reasons. First, neither wheat nor corn is usually eaten as a whole, unprocessed grain. They are milled and baked into bread, chapatis, nan, tortillas, or some other form. This not only requires more labor, but nutrients are unavoidably compromised and lost in the process. Rice, on the other hand, can be cooked as a whole grain, without processing. In addition, its amino acid composition is superior to wheat and corn, and a rice diet requires a smaller amount of supplementary nutrition from other food sources to be complete and whole.

The traditional Japanese diet combines rice with such fermented soybean products as miso, soy sauce, and natto to make for a full complement of all required amino acids. Because rice and beans are so rich in amino acids, smaller amounts can be consumed, lessening the burden on the digestive system and other internal organs. This combination of rice and beans found in the traditional Japanese diet is ideal.

In the last century, however, the Japanese diet has changed dramatically. The late Edwin O. Reischauer, professor at Harvard and former U.S. ambassador to Japan, pointed out this recently acquired failing in Japanese eating habits: "The traditional Japanese diet of rice, vegetables, and seafood is almost ideal in terms of health—or it would be, if only the Japanese could conquer their addiction to white rice with the germ and bran removed." No matter how complete rice may be as a food, it can only benefit us if we eat complete, unpolished rice.

The traditional Japanese diet, guaranteed to provide long life and health and superlative in its powers to ward off and cure disease, can be summarized in four key points:

1. The main part of the diet consists of unpolished, brown rice. Other grains and beans—barley, millet, azuki beans, black beans, and soybeans—can and should be added to the rice for variety and as nutritional supplements.

2. Leaf and root vegetables, sea vegetables, beans, fermented products (such as miso, soy sauce, and natto), and small fish and shellfish should be eaten as side dishes.

3. All seasonings should be natural and unprocessed.

4. The main rice or rice-and-grain dish should account for over half the bulk of each meal. It is important to chew thoroughly and push away from the table before completely full.

FOOD IS THE BEST MEDICINE

Most chronic illness can be traced back to a poor diet, and so improving the diet is the secret to curing such illnesses. At the same time, it is also important to use natural remedies that will alleviate symptoms and assist the body in recovering naturally. Many such natural remedies have been in use in Japan from ancient times. Devised and tested by our ancestors over long centuries, these are all very effective and safe cures that have none of the side effects of modern synthetic drugs.

Let's look at just one example of the kind of natural remedies available for the common cold—which can develop into so many other illnesses if not treated properly. First, we should drink a hot cup of pickled plum and ginger tea to provide the body with special nourishment. The properties of the pickled plum and parched tea known as bancha complement each other, soothing the stomach, and the ginger assists recovery by stimulating the metabolism. For an accompanying cough or sore throat, we can prepare a welsh onion compress or a mustard compress, or gargle with the juice of a grated daikon, or drink black bean broth. If the cold is accompanied by a fever, we can apply a compress of tofu or taro paste. Both of these foods have wonderful fever-reducing qualities, at the same time stimulating the body to eliminate poisons and impurities. While fever-reducing synthetic drugs may lower the body temperature for a time, they do not cure the root cause of the fever. The patient must keep taking the drug to suppress the symptom, but this is likely to cause side effects, such as an upset stomach.

Other natural remedies include grated daikon with a dash of soy sauce for hangover; a pickled plum pressed against the temples for a headache; a slice of raw onion for insomnia; all of these, and many other natural remedies from the Japanese kitchen, use our natural foods to correct any irregularities that occur in our systems.

The Chinese character that we use in Japan to write the word for medicine 薬 means to enjoy 楽 plants 艹 . It tells us that medicines originally derived from plants, just as our basic diet did. In fact, there is an ancient Chinese saying, "Medicines and foods grow from the same root." In China plants, especially those with a strong life force, have long been used as medicines, and the Chinese have from ancient times developed medicines and medicinal diets in tandem. This book, though partly based on that tradition, is not a manual of Chinese herbal medicine. It is a sampling of food remedies. We know that the foods we eat every day—grains, beans, vegetables, sea vegetables, and nuts—possess many different active ingredients that promote and restore health. The only effective, long-term method for preserving and increasing our health is through healthy eating.

BASIC INGREDIENTS AND TECHNIQUES

The Japanese food remedies in this book use some basic ingredients that may be unfamiliar to Western cooks, but a surprising number of them are now available in well-stocked supermarkets and health-food stores. For others, you may have to visit an Asian grocery. Fortunately, these have sprung up in large numbers all over the United States in the last decade. It probably doesn't matter whether the Asian grocery in your area is operated by Americans of Korean, Chinese, Thai, Indian, or Japanese descent—-most of the ingredients are used by more than one Asian culture.

Several of these ingredients are often prepared in a preliminary fashion before they are incorporated into recipes. For example, sheets of the sea vegetable called nori are often toasted lightly before being cut, shredded, or crumbled and then used as a garnish. Different kinds of beans must be boiled in different ways, and dried foods must be reconstituted. Those basic preliminary techniques are described with the ingredients below.

Azuki beans

These red beans are frequently used in Japanese cooking. They are rich in complex carbohydrates, B vitamins, and minerals.

To prepare boiled azuki beans, soak 1 cup of beans in 3 cups of water overnight, then boil for 30 minutes. This recipe makes 2 to 2$1/2$ cup of boiled beans.

Black beans

Common in many different Asian cuisines, black beans are a variety of soy bean. Traditionally, black beans are regarded as having many medicinal properties. They are also rich in the B vitamins, iron, and calcium.

Black beans cooked with brown rice, and soy milk made from black beans are excellent for building strength and combating allergies. Boiling black beans in an iron pot, or placing an iron nail in the pot will insure that the beans have a beautiful shiny black color after cooking.

Black beans are also prepared as black bean juice, tofu, miso, soy powder, soy sauce, and bean oil, as well as eaten, boiled and salted, in the pod.

To prepare boiled black beans, soak 1 cup of beans in 3 cups of water overnight, then boil for 30 minutes. This recipe makes 2 to $2^1/2$ cup of boiled beans

Burdock root (gobo)

Burdock is a long, thin, fibrous light brown root that is eaten only in Japan. It has an earthy taste that comes mainly from the skin, so it should not be scrubbed too roughly before cooking. A light going over with a vegetable brush is enough.

Daikon (Japanese radish)

Japanese radish is now widely available in the United States, and this long white root vegetable is very widely used in Japanese cuisine. It is grated to make sauces (mixed with soy sauce, for example, to dip sashimi), eaten raw, boiled, dried, and pickled. It is not nearly as hot as the red Western radish, but it still has a clear, sharp taste that complements oily or strongly odorous foods. It also aids digestion and warms the body. When cooked, daikon absorbs other flavors and concentrates them, making it delicious in stews and soups.

Daikon sprouts are also sold in Asian groceries and health-food stores. They are quite hot, like a Western radish.

Enoki mushrooms

These mushrooms (Flammulina veltipes) have thin, white stems and small button tops and are grown in dense clumps. Commonly available in Japanese and Asian food stores, they have a fresh taste and a crunchy texture, and they are frequently used in soups and stews.

Fried tofu (abura age)

Fried tofu is prepared by slicing tofu thinly, removing the excess water, and deep-frying the slices in soy or rapeseed oil. This makes it high in fat, and when it is used as part of a stew or soup, the excess oil should be removed first by simmering the tofu slices in hot water, draining them, and patting them dry. Fried tofu also lends itself to grilling, with a miso or soy sauce and grated ginger topping. Its unique form allows it to be cut into a sort of pocket that can then be stuffed with sushi rice or vegetables.

Garlic chives (nira)

Garlic chives are a chive with flat leaves that have a strong garlic odor and taste. They are available in Asian food stores and are wonderful in soups (they are also a major ingredient in the stuffing of the fried Chinese dumplings often called "pot stickers"). Select bunches with shorter leaves that are still tender and dark, lustrous green.

Gingko nuts

Gingko nuts are available in every Chinese grocery. You can even harvest your own in the fall. They are rich in carotene, Vitamin C, calcium, and iron, and in Japan and China are regarded as a tonic that is indispensable for vitality and long life. Fresh gingko nuts, still in the shell, are prepared by parboiling and then shucking. The nut meats should then be simmered in lightly salted water for about five minutes before being mixed with rice or vegetables. Gingko nuts are also available canned, in which case cooking is unnecessary.

Kuzu starch

The kuzu plant is a vigorous vining legume. Introduced to the American south as a natural erosion control, it has created an environmental disaster, smothering and killing native plants. The tubers of the vine are used to produce a powder called kuzu starch which is used in a variety of ways in Japanese cooking, including dumplings, cakes, and noodles. It also has medicinal uses, as a nutritional supplement for children and the elderly, as a cure for diarrhea, and in the form of a traditional herbal medicine called kakkonto, which has many uses. Kuzu starch is available in both Asian groceries and health stores. While cornstarch can be substituted as a thickener, it does not possess the same healing properties and should not be substituted in these recipes.

The secret to using kuzu powder is to combine a small amount of powder with a small amount of water first, and then stir that paste into the remaining water and powder, just as you would when using cornstarch.

Lotus root

Lotus root is actually the tuber of the lotus plant. It is crunchy, has a white skin, and can be eaten peeled or unpeeled. Lotus tuber is especially decorative when sliced, because it has a pattern of hollow areas that make each slice resemble an open flower.

Miso (fermented salty soybean paste, with or without cereals)

Miso is categorized into three types, depending upon the type of fermenting agent used. The lightly salted white miso and the much saltier Shinshu and Sendai miso use rice as the fermenting agent. The so-called "country miso" (inaka miso) uses wheat, and hatcho miso, Nagoya miso, and tamari miso use soybeans as the fermenting agent. Miso is also categorized as sweet or salty depending upon the proportions of soybeans, fermenting agent, and salt used, and by its color. There is white miso, brown miso, and red miso. In Japan, miso is also often identified by its place of origin. Miso is judged by its luster, consistency, firmness, fragrance, and taste, in particular the latter two qualities.

Miso's distinctive smell and absorbency make it excellent for masking the odor of fish. It combines well with all kinds of meat and vegetables, and can be used in soups, stews, and grilled foods alike. To savor its distinctive smell, always add it last to soups and stews. Various seasoned misos, with such additions as rice vinegar, citron peel, and roasted and ground sesame seeds, are also available.

Mountain yam (yamaimo)

The mountain yam is the rounded hairy tuber of a vine native to Japan. A cultivated form of the plant is called Yamato imo. Mountain yams consist mostly of highly digestible starch. Because they also contain amylase, polyphenolase, and oxidase, they help digest other foods eaten with them. Mountain yams have a crunchy texture and are usually prepared by grating to form a sticky paste or sauce, which ensures that the amylase functions to the fullest extent. They are best eaten raw, since the amino acids are deactivated by high cooking temperatures.

Natto

Natto is made by fermenting simmered soybeans. Fermenting the beans makes their nutrients much more readily available for digestion, and also improves the digestibility of the foods it is eaten in combination with. For many Westerners, natto is definitely an acquired taste—just as cheese is for many Asians. It is available in Asian food stores, usually in frozen packs.

Onion

The remedies and recipes in this book use two kinds of onion, ordinary yellow onions (tamanegi) and Welsh onions (negi, or naganegi). Welsh onions (Allium fistulosum) are an Asian species of onion with slender bulbs similar to green onions or spring onions but longer and larger in circumference. They are ubiquitous in traditional Japanese cooking, and finely sliced Welsh onions are one of the most common garnishes and seasonings. They can usually be found in Asian groceries, and green or spring onions can be substituted.

Pickled plums (umeboshi)

Pickled plums are a healthy snack and a wonderful way to clean the palate after eating oily or starchy foods. They are a part of every traditional Japanese lunchbox. Be careful when eating an umeboshi for the first time: the flavor is very concentrated and extremely tart. They are available in Japanese food stores. Many of the recipes in this book call for pickled plum meat. Simply remove the pit and shred or dice the pickled plum.

Pickled shiso leaves (ume shiso)

Shiso leaves are either red or green. Red shiso is used in making pickled plums, and it gives the plums their deep red coloring. The leaves are also delicious chopped and mixed with cooked rice or sushi rice. Pickled shiso leaves are available in Asian food stores.

Pickles

Pickles have long been a part of the Japanese diet, and there are more than five hundred varieties made in Japan. They are enjoyed for their light taste, which cleans the palate; their refreshing fragrance, which stimulates the appetite; and their crunchy texture. Almost all pickles are made from vegetables, making themn a source of vitamins, minerals, and dietary fiber. They are the perfect snack food.

Japanese pickles are made by fermenting in rice bran and saltwater, or simply by marinating them in salt or miso for a few hours. Fermented pickles rely on the activity of aerobic bacteria, so they must be stirred once or twice a day. Pickles that are ready in just a short time, from a few hours to overnight, retain most of their vitamins.

Pumpkin

Japanese pumpkins are much smaller than those commonly seen in the United States. They are similar in size the acorn squash, which can be substituted.

Sake and mirin

Both of these alcoholic beverages are distilled from rice. Ordinary sake, available at most liquor stores, is fine for cooking. Mirin is a sweet rice wine, somewhat similar to sherry. They are used in small amounts as flavorings and marinades.

Sea vegetables

Sea vegetables (also called seaweed) are widely used in Japanese cooking and a variety are available at Japanese food stores. Aonori is usually seen as fine flakes, packaged in a cellophane envelope. It is convenient for sprinkling over foods as a garnish. Hijiki is a stringy dark brown or black algae that can be purchased in a wet pack or dried. To reconstitute dried hijiki, simply soak it in enough water to cover it for about 20 minutes.

Nori is a dark green seaweed, the kind used to make sushi rolls. It is sold in large square sheets, and it is usually toasted over an open flame before using, which improves its flavor. To toast nori, hold a sheet high enough above the flame to keep it from igniting, and briefly pass it evenly over the heat, one side as a time. If you look closely, you will see the nori change color slightly as it toasts. Nori is shredded by hand or cut into strips with scissors to use as a garnish. You can make large nori flakes by lightly toasting both sides of a sheet of nori over a flame, then placing the sheet in a plastic bag and crumpling it into large irregular flakes. To make nori strips, toast the nori and then use scissors to cut it into thin strips about 1 1/2 inches long. You can also purchase nori already cut into strips, but it tastes better if you prepare it yourself.

Kombu is a large kelp leaf, used in making soup stock. It, too, must be reconstituted by soaking in water for about 20 minutes. Before adding the kombu to the stock, cut fringes along its edges, increasing the surface area that will come into contact with the water.

Sesame, black & white

Sesame is a delicious and ubiquitous flavoring of Japanese cooking. Sesame-based foods, sauces, and condiments include sesame salt, parched sesame seeds, ground sesame seeds, chopped sesame seeds, sesame tofu, sesame sauce, sesame miso, sesame vinegar, sesame soy sauce, sesame dipping sauce, sesame paste, sesame sweets, and many foods deep fried in sesame oil. Rich in vitamins and minerals and attributed with a wide variety of medicinal effects, sesame is called "the wonderful herb of long life" in the East. Black sesame seeds have a stronger effect than white.

Two commonly used sesame-based ingredients are sesame paste and sesame salt. Sesame paste is available in Asian food stores and some natural food stores, but you can easily make your own by roasting 1 cup of sesame seeds in a pan until they begin to release their oil, then grinding them in a mortar for 5 minutes until smooth. This recipe will make 1/2 cup of paste.

Sesame salt is available already prepared in health food stores and Asian groceries, or you can make it yourself. In a heavy frying pan saute 1 teaspoon of sea salt, being careful not to burn it, for about 3 minutes. Place it in a mortar and grind fine. Heat up the pan again and saute the 10 tablespoons of black sesame seeds, 5 tablespoons at a time, for about 1 minute over medium heat, until they are fragrant. Add the sesame seeds to the mortar and grind lightly for about 5 minutes. After the mixture has cooled, place it in a jar. It should be used within 4 or 5 days.

Shiitake

Shiitake mushrooms are perhaps the most widely used in Japanese cooking and most large supermarkets in the United States now stock them both fresh and dried. Shiitake are appreciated for both their flavor and their fragrance, and have traditionally been regarded as useful in fighting colds and clearing mucous membranes. Rich in vitamin D and low in calories, they assist the body's metabolization of waste products and are effective in helping to control obesity, diabetes, and kidney disease, as well as such psychological symptoms as nervousness and apathy. Recently, shiitake have been found to contain chemicals that lower cholesterol, and they are now being analyzed for natural anticarcinogens.

Fresh shiitake are best eaten grilled and sprinkled with a little salt and then dipped in a vinegar-citrus sauce, or sauteed and served sprinkled with lemon juice. Their rich flavor is an excellent contribution to rice dishes and stews. Dried shiitake make wonderful soup stock, because their flavor is more concentrated. Shiitake are reconstituted by placing them in enough water to cover them and let them soak for about twenty minutes. When reconstituting shiitake, it's important not to leave them in water too long, for they will gradually lose their flavor. It's also an excellent idea to use the water they've been soaked in as soup stock.

Shimeji

Shimeji (Lyophyllum aggregatum) are small brown button-headed mushrooms that grow in a cluster. They have a slippery texture and a nutty taste and are excellent in soups and stews. They are widely available in Japanese food stores.

Soy sauce

Soy sauce is produced by fermenting water, salt, and a yeast made from soybeans and wheat for about one year. There are three main kinds. The saltier koikuchi soy sauce is fermented for a longer period and is thick. The less salty, or light usukuchi soy sauce is fermented for a shorter time. The variety known as tamari is sweeter than the others. Artificially brewed soy sauce, which uses amino acids and chemical processes to sidestep the natural brewing period, is now available, but it lacks the flavor, nutrition, and medicinal properties of the real thing. Soy sauce not only seasons with salt but complements and accentuates the taste of fats and oils in food. It is combined with other seasonings and flavorings to create many varieties of flavored and medicinal soy sauces.

When flavoring clear soups with soy sauce, it should be added at the last minute, so that its flavor and smell are preserved. In stews it helps prevent the ingredients from falling apart, so it should be added at the beginning, with a small amount added at the last moment as seasoning. Soy sauce is also used on grilled and braised foods, upon which it forms an appetizing deep brown glaze with a delicious aroma.

In general, salty soy sauce is used in cooking, light soy sauce is used when preserving the natural flavors and colors of the ingredients is important, and tamari is used for dipping raw fish fillets (sashimi).

Soup stock (dashi)

To prepare a Japanese vegetarian soup stock, place 5 cups of mineral water in a pan. Wash a 4-inch square of kombu, and cut a fringe of 5 or 6 lines on each of its edges. Add the kombu and 3 reconstituted shiitake to the water and simmer for 30 minutes. Remove the shiitake and kombu.

Soybeans

Soybeans are ubiquitous in Japanese cooking. They are eaten in their pods, boiled and salted, as a snack with beer or cold drinks in the summer. They are simmered in a bean stew, sprinkled in pow-dered form over rice and rice cakes, and are the main ingredients of such basic Japanese foodstuffs as tofu, natto, miso, and soy sauce. Though soybeans are rich in protein and nutrients, they are not easily digestible in whole form, but are much more so as miso and tofu (95%).

Soybean sprouts are readily available in many food stores, but you can easily sprout them yourself by placing 1 cup of dried soybeans in about 3 cups of water and letting them soak for ten hours. Rinse them lightly and drain them. Spread the beans out in a large strainer or pan lined with white paper towel and wrap it in a plastic bag. Make 1 or 2 air holes in the bag for ventilation. Twice a day, open the bag and sprinkle a little water over the beans to keep them damp. The beans should sprout on about the third day. When the sprouts are about as long as the bean itself, they are ready to use.

Taro
Taro is now widely available in U.S. supermarkets, since it is a staple of much Latin American and Caribbean cooking.

Tofu
Tofu is widely available in grocery stores all over the United States.

Welsh onion
See Onion.

Vinegars
Japanese cooking uses vinegar as a flavoring in many dishes. Always try to have rice vinegar and plum vinegar (umesu) on hand. Apple vinegar can be substituted in a pinch.

INDEX OF SYMPTOMS AND CONDITIONS

The alphabetical list of symptoms and conditions refers the reader to the ingredients that are traditionally believed to alleviate each particular problem. Turn to the ingredient in the main section of the book, and try one or more of the recipes employing it.

Remember, these are traditional, natural remedies, primarily foods that should be part of the daily diet. Because they are natural, food-based remedies, they generally act slowly and gently. They are not drugs or instant cures; they are foods that work to correct imbalances in your system which are caused by poor diet, or to boost your body's natural immune functions by providing it with the complete nutrition it requires to fight disease on its own.

FOR ANY SERIOUS, ACUTE, OR PERSISTENT CONDITION, ALWAYS CONSULT YOUR DOCTOR.

Aging
Soy beans, sesame, lotus root, pickled plum, and tofu help slow the aging process and reduce suffering from the symptoms of aging.

Allergies
Black beans, onion, pickled plums, sea vegetables, garlic chives.

Anemia
Brown rice, buckwheat, sesame, garlic, garlic chives, sea vegetables, spinach, carrots.

Anti-Carcinogens
Brown rice, shiitake mushrooms, natto, garlic, pickled plums.

Appetite
Ginger, pickled plum, pickles, natto, and garlic all stimulate the appetite.

Arteriosclerosis
Brown rice, buckwheat, garlic, shiitake mushrooms, sea vegetables, and tofu are effective in preventing and treating hardening of the arteries.

Asthma
Gingko nuts, ginger, lotus root, pickled plums.

Bedwetting
Garlic chives, mountain yam, ginko nuts, and sesame can reduce urination during the night.

Bloating
Burdock, azuki beans, pumpkin.

Chills
Brown rice, garlic, garlic chives, kuzu, carrots.

Circulatory system
Onion, brown rice, natto, sea vegetables, and spinach are excellent tonics for the circulatory system.

Colds and flu
Ginger, onion, kuzu, shiitake mushrooms, pumpkin, lotus root, pickled plums, garlic chives, welsh onion, garlic, soybeans, daikon, carrot.

Constipation
Brown rice, buckwheat, sesame, daikon, sea vegetables, taro, burdock.

Coughs
Gingko nuts, daikon, ginger, lotus root.

Diabetes
Millet, soy beans, onion, shiitake mushrooms, pumpkin, and tofu help control blood sugar levels and diabetes.

Diarrhea
Ginger, garlic, garlic chives, mountain yam.

Digestion

Garlic, mountain yam, daikon and pickled plum promote good digestion and the health of the digestive tract.

Fever

Taro, tofu, shiitake, ginger.

Goiter

Sea vegetables.

Hair

Sesame seeds and sea vegetables can prevent graying hair and welsh onions and ginger can help prevent hair loss.

Hangover

Daikon, lotus root, pickled plum, miso.

Headache

Pickled plum, sesame, azuki beans, carrot, lotus root.

Heart disease

Brown rice, soy beans, garlic, lotus root, spinach, sea vegetables, and tofu both help prevent and treat the aftereffects of heart disease.

Hemorrhoids

Sesame, garlic, garlic chives.

Hiccups

Ginger (warm ginger juice), lotus root.

High blood pressure

Buckwheat, sesame, daikon, sea vegetables, lotus root, tofu, shiitake.

Hoarseness

Black beans, daikon, lotus root.

Hot flashes

Daikon combats hot flashes and sudden flushing of the face.

Infertility

Brown rice, soybeans, sesame, miso, natto.

Intestinal ailments

Garlic chives, natto.

Intestinal parasites

Buckwheat, garlic, garlic chives, pickled plums, welsh onion.

Kidney ailments
Azuki beans, sesame, sea vegetables, pumpkin, black beans, burdock, spinach.

Liver ailments
Onion, garlic, shiitake mushrooms, miso, tofu, natto, garlic chives, brown rice, welsh onion.

Low blood pressure
Carrots, brown rice, grains, pickled plums, spinach.

Menopause symptoms
Lotus root, spinach, pickled plum, burdock.

Milk production (in nursing mothers)
Brown rice, soy beans, sesame, azuki beans, mountain yam.

Motion sickness
Pickled plum, kuzu, spinach.

Nausea
Ginger (warm ginger juice).

Nerve ailments
Sesame, kuzu, taro, spinach, pickled plums, sea vegetables, tofu, lotus root, ginger, sesame.

Nervousness and irritability
Brown rice, sea vegetables, mountain yam, lotus root, onion, carrot.

Night blindness
Carrots, sesame, spinach, pumpkin.

Obesity
Brown rice, shiitake mushrooms, sea vegetables, natto, tofu.

Phlegm and congestion
Black beans, gingko nuts, shiitake mushrooms, burdock, daikon.

Physical and mental energizer
Brown rice, millet, black beans, spinach.

Prostrate health
Pumpkin, kuzu.

Radiation exposure
Natto, miso.

Rashes
Garlic chives, welsh onion.

Reproductive organ dysfunctions
Mountain yam, sea vegetables, brown rice.

Retarded growth and development
Sea vegetables, pumpkin, brown rice, soybeans.

Sexual vigor
Daikon, garlic chives, mountain yam, lotus root, burdock, natto.

Sinusitis
Garlic, kuzu, sesame, sea vegetables, natto, lotus root, pickled plums.

Skin problems and conditioning
Garlic chives, pumpkin, spinach, carrots.

Sleep disorders
Garlic chives, onion, garlic, welsh onion.

Sore throat
Black beans, daikon, lotus root.

Stamina
Onion, brown rice, black beans, sesame, mountain yam.

Stomach ailments
Ginger, kuzu, pickled plum, spinach, miso, mountain yam.

Stress
Pickled plum, brown rice, sesame.

Tiredness
Tea, pickled plum, carrots, azuki beans, kuzu.

Urinary functions
Sesame, garlic chives, burdock, azuki beans, ginko.

Weakness
Carrots, brown rice, black beans, sea vegetables, lotus root, burdock.

RECIPES

**SIMMERED AZUKI BEANS
WITH LOTUS ROOT**

AZUKI BEANS

For constipation, asthma, chills, diarrhea, headache, sore throat, bloating, kidney disease, anemia, weakness, tiredness. They also encourage milk production in nursing mothers, promote sexual vigor and healthy skin, stimulate the appetite, and help the body rid itself of toxins and impurities.

SIMMERED AZUKI BEANS WITH LOTUS ROOT

$1/2$ cup boiled azuki beans (page 16)
$1/2$ fresh lotus root
2 cups soup stock (page 23)
1 pickled plum
4 inches kombu for stock
1 tablespoon salt
2 tablespoons pumpkin

Cut the lotus root into $1/8$-inch slices. Cut the kombu into $1/2$-inch squares and combine the lotus root, kombu, pickled plum, and soup stock in a pan and simmer for 15 minutes, until the vegetables are tender. Add the boiled azuki beans and simmer another 4 to 5 minutes. Add the salt. Cut the pumpkin unpeeled into $1/2$-inch cubes and boil in lightly salted water for 5 minutes. Place the bean mixture in a serving dish and garnish with the pumpkin.

AZUKI AND WHEAT TREATS

$2/3$ cup dry azuki beans
4 cups water
$1/4$ cup wheat berries
$2/3$ cup unrefined brown sugar
1 tablespoon salt
4 squares of dried rice cake (mochi)

Place the azuki beans in 1½ cups water and boil for 5 minutes, then drain. Wash the wheat berries and add 2 cups of boiling water, then soak for about 1 hour. Drain. Place the beans in a pressure cooker and add 4 cups water. Seal the lid and cook over medium heat until pressurized, then reduce heat to low and cook 10 minutes. Remove from heat and allow to depressurize. While waiting, toast the rice cakes in a skillet or over a grill until lightly browned on both sides. After opening the pressure cooker lid, add the drained wheat berries and simmer without the lid for 10 minutes. Add the brown sugar and salt and stir. Place in a bowl and top with toasted rice cakes.

AZUKI BEAN SUSHI

---

3 cups brown rice
3½ cups water
1 teaspoon tumeric
4 inches kombu for stock
⅓ cup vinegar
1 tablespoon salt
1 tablespoon honey
1 cup boiled azuki beans (page 16)
10 snow peas
½ small carrot

Place the rice, water, tumeric, and kombu in a pressure cooker and place over high heat until pressurized. Reduce heat to low and cook for 20 minutes. Remove from heat and allow to depressurize. Open the lid and move the rice to a low, flat pan or tub. Combine the vinegar, salt, and honey and sprinkle over the rice, folding it in with a flat bamboo rice paddle, spatula, or a wooden spoon. Parboil the snow peas in lightly salted water for 1 minute. Drain and cut into small, attractive slices. Cut the carrots into ⅛-inch slices, then quarter the slices and parboil for 1 minute in lightly salted water. Toss the vegetables into the rice mixture, add the boiled azuki beans, and serve.

AZUKI BEAN
SUSHI

BLACK BEANS WITH GRATED APPLE

BLACK BEANS

For sore throat, phlegm, allergies, asthma, diabetes, kidney ailments, anemia, high blood pressure, and constipation. They also increase physical and sexual vigor, stimulate the appetite, promote healthy skin, and rid the system of toxins and impurities.

BLACK BEANS SIMMERED WITH KOMBU

1 cup black beans
6 inches kombu
6 cups water
2/3 cup unrefined brown sugar
2 tablespoons soy sauce

Place the black beans in a pressure cooker and soak in 3 cups of water for 8 hours. Add the kombu, and cook over high heat until pressurized, then turn the heat to low and cook for 10 minutes. Remove from heat and allow to depressurize. Open the lid and add the sugar and soy sauce. Simmer in the open pressure cooker for 4 to 5 minutes.

BLACK BEANS WITH GRATED APPLE

1/2 cup boiled black beans (page 17)
1/2 apple, grated
1 tablespoon vinegar
1 teaspoon salt

Dress the boiled beans with the apple, vinegar, and salt, and serve.

BLACK BEAN RICE

---

¹/₂ cup black beans
2 cups brown rice
3¹/₂ cups water
sesame salt for seasoning

Place the black beans in a frying pan and gently roast them, taking care not to burn them, over medium heat for 3 to 4 minutes until fragrant. Place the brown rice and roasted beans in a pressure cooker and add the water. Place over high heat until pressurized, then lower the heat to medium and cook for 20 minutes. Remove from heat and allow to depressurize. Serve, sprinkled with sesame salt.

BROWN RICE

For constipation, heart disease, arteriosclerosis, stomach ailments, low blood pressure, obesity, nervousness and irritability, anemia, and infertility. It also helps prevent miscarriages, promotes sexual and mental vigor, acts as a tonic for the circulatory system, and has been shown to countereffect the harm caused by environmental pollution and to suppress cancer.

BROWN RICE WITH MIXED GRAINS

1¹/₂ cups brown rice
¹/₅ cup pearl barley
¹/₅ cup azuki beans
¹/₅ cup black beans
²/₅ cup millet
¹/₂ teaspoon sea salt
3 cups water

BROWN RICE
WITH MIXED
GRAINS

**BROWN RICE
PORRIDGE**

Mix all the grains together, wash thoroughly, and drain. Place the grains in a pressure cooker with the water and let the mixture sit for 5 hours. Then add the salt, seal the pressure cooker lid, and place the pressure cooker on high heat until it is pressurized. Then turn the heat to low and cook for 20 minutes. After finished cooking, let the cooker sit with the lid on for 15 minutes. Remove the lid and stir once or twice before serving.

BROWN RICE PORRIDGE

1 cup brown rice
6 cups water
1/2 teaspoon salt
sesame salt (page 22) as needed

Wash the brown rice thoroughly and drain it. Place it in a pressure cooker with the water and salt and let the mixture stand for at least 5 hours. Seal the pressure cooker lid and place the cooker on high heat until pressurized. Then turn the heat to low and cook for 30 minutes. After finished cooking, let the cooker sit with the lid on for 20 minutes. Remove the lid and season the porridge with salt. Serve in soup bowls and sprinkle with sesame salt.

BROWN RICE CREAM

1 cup brown rice
8 cups water
2/3 teaspoon salt
sesame salt and pickled plums as needed

Wash the brown rice thoroughly and drain it. Place it in a pressure cooker and toast the rice lightly and evenly over high heat, about 10 minutes. Add the water and salt, seal the pressure cooker lid, and cook over high heat until pressurized. Then turn the heat down to low and cook for thirty minutes. After the rice is finished cooking, let the cooker sit with the lid on for 20 minutes. Remove the lid and place the cooked rice mixture in a blender. Blend until smooth, then add more salt if necessary. Serve the hot mixture in soup bowls and sprinkle with sesame salt. Eat with the pickled plums.

BUCKWHEAT

For constipation, high blood pressure, anemia, intestinal parasites, and arteriosclerosis. It also promotes healthy skin.

Japanese buckwheat noodles, or soba, are sold in small bundles, usually several bundles to a pack. Most soba noodles are not one hundred percent buckwheat, but also contain wheat flour, which helps the noodles hold together. For these food remedies to be most effective, use noodles with the highest percentage of buckwheat you can find.

BROWN RICE
CREAM

**BUCKWHEAT NOODLES
WITH VEGETABLES**

BUCKWHEAT NOODLES WITH VEGETABLES

1 bundle dried buckwheat noodles

4 dried shiitake mushrooms (page 22)

1 tablespoon soy sauce

1 tablespoon mirin

3 cups bean sprouts

1 medium carrot

2 Japanese cucumbers (or small, thin Western cucumbers)

2 welsh onions, sliced into very thin rounds

4 tablespoons soy sauce

4 tablespoons vinegar

2 tablespoons mirin

2 tablespoons sake

^{1}/3 cup ground white sesame seeds

1 welsh onion, sliced thinly

^{1}/3 cup soup stock (page 23)

Chinese mustard as needed, for seasoning

Reconstitute the shiitake, then chop them into matchsticks. Add the soy sauce and the mirin to ^{1}/3 cup of soup stock and simmer the chopped shiitake in this mixture for 10 minutes. Parboil the bean sprouts for about 1 minute. Drain them and sprinkle them with a little salt and pepper. Chop the carrot into matchsticks and simmer them in lightly salted water for 3 minutes. Slice the cucumber thinly at an angle and then chop the slices into matchsticks.

Combine the soy sauce, vinegar, sake, ground white sesame seeds, thinly sliced welsh onion rounds, and soup stock to create the sauce to be poured over the noodles later.

Place the soba in plenty of vigorously boiling water. When the water returns to a boil, pour in a cup of cold water, and when it comes to a boil again, drain the noodles, rinse them in cold water, and shake out as much moisture as possible.

Place the noodles in a large bowl (or individual bowls) and sprinkle with the vegetables, including the remaining thinly sliced welsh onion. Pour the sauce gently over the mixture. Place a dab of Chinese mustard paste on the side of the dish to mix in as you eat.

BUCKWHEAT NOODLES WITH GRATED MOUNTAIN YAM DRESSING

1 1/2 bundles dried buckwheat noodles
1/2 mountain yam
1 cup soup stock (page 23)
1/3 cup soy sauce
1/3 cup mirin
1 sheet toasted seaweed cut into thin strips about 1 inch long (page 21)
2 finely sliced welsh onions
2 tablespoons pine nuts
minced chili pepper for seasoning

Combine the soup stock, soy sauce, and mirin. Bring to a boil and then allow to cool. This will be the dipping sauce for the noodles.

Burn off the hairy fibers protruding from the skin of the mountain yam by singing it lightly over a flame, then grate the yam without peeling it.

Boil the buckwheat noodles for four minutes in plenty of boiling water. Remove, drain, and shake out as much water as possible.

Serve the noodles in a dish, topping them with the grated mountain yam and sprinkling the seaweed, thinly sliced welsh onion, and pine nuts over the whole. Dip the noodles in the dipping sauce as you eat.

**BUCKWHEAT NOODLES
WITH GRATED
MOUNTAIN YAM
DRESSING**

BUCKWHEAT
NOODLE SALAD

1 bunch dried buckwheat noodles
1/5 medium daikon
1/3 small carrot
1 bunch daikon sprouts
1 sheet toasted seaweed cut into thin strips about 1 inch long (page 21)
4 tablespoons soy sauce
3 tablespoons vinegar
3 tablespoons mirin
1 tablespoon sesame oil
3 tablespoons ground sesame seed

Cut the daikon and the carrot into matchsticks and sprinkle a little salt on each. Cut the daikon sprouts in half.

Boil the buckwheat noodles in plenty of water for 4 minutes. Drain, rinse, and shake out as much water as possible.

Mix the daikon, carrot, and noodles and serve in a dish. Sprinkle the seaweed strips over the noodles. Combine the soy sauce, vinegar, mirin, sesame oil, and ground sesame seed, and sprinkle over the noodle mixture as a dressing.

BURDOCK

For constipation, urinary problems, arteriosclerosis, bloating, anemia, uterine infections, asthma, hemorrhoids, high blood pressure, kidney ailments, low blood pressure, sore throat, and phlegm. It also promotes physical and sexual vigor and rids the system of toxins and impurities.

BURDOCK JULIENNE

1/2 burdock
1/2 small carrot
1/2 fresh ginger root
1/2 cup soup stock (page 23)
3 tablespoons soy sauce
2 teaspoons mirin
1 tablespoon sake
1 tablespoon white sesame seeds

Cut the burdock, carrot, and ginger by slicing thinly at an angle, and then cutting the slices into matchsticks (julienne). Place them in a pot and add the soup stock. Simmer for 4 to 5 minutes. Add the soy sauce, mirin, and sake, and simmer for another 5 to 6 minutes, until all the liquid is absorbed. Serve and garnish with the white sesame seeds.

SIMMERED BURDOCK

1 burdock
4 inches kombu for stock
3 cups soup stock (page 23)
1/4 cup soy sauce
2 tablespoons sake
2 tablespoons mirin
1/2 chili pepper
seaweed flakes for garnish

Cut the burdock into 4-inch lengths. Place the soup stock in a pot, add the kombu and the burdock, and simmer for 20 minutes, until the burdock is tender. Add the soy sauce, mirin, and chili pepper and continue simmering until the liquid is absorbed. Cut the burdock into bite-size pieces and serve garnished with the seaweed flakes.

**BURDOCK
JULIENNE**

**BURDOCK
WITH MISO**

BURDOCK WITH MISO

²/₃ burdock
¹/₂ cup white miso
I tablespoon mirin
I tablespoon sake
2 tablespoons sesame paste (page 22)
thinly sliced welsh onion for garnish

Cut the burdock at an angle into large, bite-size pieces. Boil in water with a dash of vinegar for about 10 minutes, until tender. Drain and pat dry. Prepare a dressing by mixing together the white miso, mirin, sake, and sesame paste. Pour the dressing over the burdock, garnish with the thinly sliced welsh onions, and serve.

CARROT

For allergies, asthma, bedwetting, anemia, chills, colds and flu, constipation, diabetes, headache, heart disease, high blood pressure, kidney ailments, liver ailments, low blood pressure, nervousness and irritability, sore throat, stomach ailments, weakness, lack of stamina, tiredness, and night blindness. They also promote healthy skin and act as a tonic for the circulatory system.

CARROT RICE

I¹/₂ carrots
2 cups cooked brown rice
2 cups water
¹/₂ teaspoon salt
minced parsley as a garnish

Mince the carrot and simmer in 2 cups of lightly salted water for 3 minutes. Drain the carrots well and fold, with the salt, into the rice. Garnish with parsley and serve.

GLAZED CARROTS

2 carrots
8 prunes
minced parsley for garnish
1 1/2 cups soup stock (page 23)
1/4 cup mirin
2 tablespoons plum vinegar

Cut the carrots into 1-inch slices and square off the edges. Combine the carrots, prunes, soup stock, mirin, and plum vinegar in a pot and simmer until the liquid is absorbed. Serve and garnish with parsley.

CARROT AND NATTO SALAD

1 small carrot
1 pack natto
1 welsh onion
1 tablespoon soy sauce
1 tablespoon sesame seeds
2 tablespoons vinegar

Cut the carrot into matchsticks and simmer in 2 cups lightly salted water for 2 minutes. Drain. Mix the carrots and natto in a bowl. Mix the soy sauce, sesame seeds, and vinegar and dress over the carrots and natto.

GLAZED
CARROTS

SIMMERED
DAIKON
SLICES

DAIKON

For allergies, arteriosclerosis, asthma, colds and flu, liver ailments, low blood pressure, phlegm and congestion, stomach ailments, hot flashes and flushing, constipation, high blood pressure, coughs, sore throat, hoarseness, hangover, toothache. It also promotes sexual vigor and healthy skin.

DAIKON TEA

1/3 cup grated daikon
2 teaspoons grated ginger root
1–2 tablespoons soy sauce
1 1/2 cup bancha tea

This is effective for reducing fever and counteracting food poisoning from meat or fish. Grate the unpeeled daikon and the ginger. Combine all the ingredients and drink.

SIMMERED DAIKON SLICES

2/3 daikon
3 tablespoons refined flour
1/2 cup hatcho miso
1/3 cup soup stock (page 23)
1/3 cup mirin
2 tablespoons sake
grated fresh ginger root as needed

Cut the daikon into round slices 1 1/2 inches thick. Place the slices in a pot with just enough water to cover them. Sprinkle the flour over the daikon slices. Simmer for about 15 minutes, until the slices are soft.

Combine the miso, soup stock, mirin, and sake in a pan and bring the mixture to a boil. Place the hot daikon slices on a serving dish, pour the miso mixture over them, and garnish with shredded fresh ginger root.

THREE-COLOR DAIKON FLOWERS

$^1/_5$ daikon
I teaspoon honey
$^2/_3$ tablespoon plum vinegar
$^1/_2$ teaspoon salt
$^1/_2$ tablespoon honey
$^1/_2$ cup vinegar
$^1/_3$ teaspoon tumeric powder
$^1/_2$ teaspoon salt
$^1/_2$ tablespoon honey
$^1/_2$ cup vinegar
chili peppers
citrus peel
green garnish

Cut the daikon into round slices I $^1/_4$ inches thick and cut them as shown in the drawing, into decorative chrysanthemum blossoms.

Divide the daikon pieces into three portions.

Prepare the pink daikon slices by adding I teaspoon of honey to the plum vinegar. Marinate $^1/_3$ of the daikon flowers in this mixture for 10 minutes.

Prepare the white daikon flowers by sprinkling $^1/_2$ teaspoon of salt over $^1/_3$ of the slices. Let them sit for a while and then remove excess water by wrapping them in a towel and pressing gently. Marinate the slices in $^1/_2$ cup of vinegar and $^1/_2$ tablespoon of honey for 10 minutes.

Prepare the yellow daikon flowers by tossing the remaining $^1/_3$ of

**THREE-COLOR
DAIKON FLOWERS**

GRATED DAIKON
WITH MUSHROOMS
AND CHIVES

the slices in tumeric powder and salt. Then marinate in $^1/_2$ cup of vinegar and $^1/_2$ tablespoon of honey for 10 minutes.

Place the flowers in a bowl and garnish with chili pepper, citrus peels, and green garnish.

GRATED DAIKON WITH MUSHROOMS AND CHIVES

$^1/_2$ pack shimeji mushrooms
$^2/_3$ tablespoon sake
$^1/_2$ teaspoon salt
$^1/_5$ daikon
1$^1/_3$ tablespoons lemon juice
$^1/_2$ teaspoon salt
1 tablespoon mirin
2 thinly sliced welsh onions

Break the clumps of shimeji mushrooms up and place in a pot with $^2/_3$ tablespoon of sake and $^1/_2$ teaspoon of salt. Place over high heat and steam for 3 minutes. Grate the daikon and place it in a strainer. Press out excess liquid. Combine the shimeji and daikon and dress with the lemon juice, salt, and mirin. Sprinkle the thinly sliced welsh onions over the mixture.

GARLIC

For stomach ailments, digestive ailments, chills, asthma, hemorrhoids, intestinal parasites, bacterial enteritis, colds and flu, sleep disorders, weakness, bloody diarrhea, heart disease, arteriosclerosis, liver ailments, sinusitis, and anemia. It also has anti-carcinogenic properties, is a tonic for the circulatory system, and an appetite stimulant.

ROASTED GARLIC WITH MISO SAUCE

1 head garlic
1 1/2 tablespoons miso
1 teaspoon sake
1 teaspoon mirin
1 teaspoon vinegar
1/5 teaspoon poppy seeds

Peel the garlic and roast in a heavy pan without oil for 3 to 4 minutes, until lightly browned. Combine the miso, sake, mirin, and vinegar in a pot and stir well. Pour over the roasted garlic. Garnish with poppy seeds.

GARLIC PICKLED IN SOY SAUCE

2 heads garlic
1/3 cup soy sauce
1 tablespoon mirin

Peel the garlic and place it in a glass bottle. Pour the soy sauce and mirin into the bottle, put on the lid, and shake, so that all of the garlic is covered. Marinate for at least 10 minutes, but the longer the better. The soy sauce marinade also makes an excellent dressing for other foods.

GARLIC CHIVES

For intestinal ailments, allergies, chills, colds and flu, intestinal parasites, liver ailments, low blood pressure, weakness, anemia, sleeplessness, chronic diarrhea, stomach ailments, chills, bedwetting, poor blood clotting, and hemorrhoids. Garlic chives also increase sexual vigor.

ROASTED GARLIC
WITH MISO SAUCE

GARLIC CHIVES
TOSSED WITH
CARROT AND ONION

GARLIC CHIVES TOSSED WITH CARROT AND ONION

I bunch garlic chives
1 1/2 inches carrot
1/2 onion
2–3 shredded pickled plums (with pits removed)
I teaspoon mirin

Cut the garlic chives into 1 1/2-inch lengths and the carrots into matchsticks. Slice the onion thinly and boil each of the three vegetables separately for 1 minute in lightly salted water. Mix the shredded pickled plums and mirin and toss the vegetables in the dressing.

GARLIC CHIVES WITH TOFU AND MISO

I bunch garlic chives
1 1/2 inches carrot
1/4 block tofu
2 tablespoons white miso
2 teaspoons mirin
3 tablespoons white sesame seeds

Cut the garlic chives into 1-inch pieces and parboil them for 30 seconds. Cut the carrots into matchsticks and boil them for 1 minute in lightly salted water. Place the tofu in a pot with just enough water to cover it and simmer for 5 minutes. Drain and shake out any excess water. Parch the white sesame seeds in a hot pan and then grind them in a mortar. Add the tofu, white miso, and mirin to the mortar and stir. Finally, add the carrots and garlic chives, and serve.

GARLIC CHIVES SOUP

1 bunch garlic chives
2 shiitake mushrooms
3 cups soup stock (page 23)
1 teaspoon salt
2 tablespoons sake
2 tablespoons mirin

Cut the garlic chives into 1-inch slices. Cut the shiitake into thin match-sticks. Combine the soup stock, salt, sake, and mirin in a pot and bring to a boil. Add the shiitake and simmer for 2 to 3 minutes. Then add the garlic chives and bring to a boil again. Remove from heat and serve.

GINGER

For poor appetite, coughs, fever, diarrhea, stomach pains, thinning hair, nerve ailments, colds and flu, nausea, hiccups, stomach upset caused by overeating, and asthma attacks.

GINGER PICKLED IN VINEGAR AND HONEY

5 fresh ginger roots
1/2 cup sake
1 tablespoon honey
1 teaspoon salt

Slice the ginger into very thin slices then toss into boiling water. Boil for about 30 seconds, then drain and press out any excess water. Marinate the ginger slices in the vinegar and honey for at least 10 minutes, longer if possible.

GINGER
PICKLED IN VINEGAR
AND HONEY

GINGKO NUTS
WITH PICKLED
PLUMS

GINGER WITH MISO

1 fresh ginger root
1 cup miso
1 1/3 tablespoons sake
1 1/3 tablespoons mirin

Mince the unpeeled ginger root and combine with the other ingredients. Stir for about 5 minutes.

GINGER SYRUP

3 cups water
1 fresh ginger root
2 tablespoons kuzu powder
3 tablespoons unrefined brown sugar

Grate the ginger root and combine all the ingredients. Bring to a boil, stirring constantly, and serve.

GINGKO NUTS

For asthma, coughs, and phlegm.

GINGKO NUTS WITH PICKLED PLUMS

1/2 cup shelled gingko nuts
2–3 shredded pickled plums (with pits removed)

Simmer the gingko nuts 5 minutes in lightly salted water, then drain and toss with the shredded pickled plums.

$^1/_2$ cup shelled gingko nuts
2 tablespoons white miso
I tablespoon sake
I tablespoon mirin
1–2 shredded pickled plums (with pits removed)

Simmer the gingko nuts for 5 minutes in lightly salted water, then drain and toss with the miso, sake, and mirin. Sprinkle with bits of shredded plum.

KUZU

For chills, stomach ailments, colds and flu, measles, pneumonia, nerve inflammation, sinusitis, and ear infections.

KUZU TONIC

I teaspoon kuzu powder
$^3/_4$ cup water
2 teaspoons unrefined brown sugar or I teaspoon honey
I teaspoon fresh ginger juice

Place the kuzu powder in a pot and slowly add the water. As with any thickener, it helps to dissolve a small amount of the powder in water first, then add the rest of the water and thickener. Cook, stirring constantly, over medium heat until the mixture comes to a boil. It will become clear at this point. Remove from heat, add the sugar or honey and the ginger juice. Drink while hot.

GINGKO NUTS
WITH MISO

KUZU SYRUP
WITH DAIKON,
CARROTS, AND
WELSH ONION

KUZU SYRUP WITH DAIKON, CARROTS, AND WELSH ONION

1/5 daikon
1/3 small carrot
4 cups soup stock (page 23)
2 tablespoons sake
1 teaspoon salt
1 tablespoon light soy sauce
2 tablespoons kuzu powder
2 tablespoons water
2 thinly sliced welsh onions

Cut the daikon and carrot into sticks. Place the soup stock and the daikon and carrot sticks in a pot and simmer for 5 minutes. When the vegetables are tender, add the sake, salt, and light soy sauce. Mix the kuzu powder and water and add to the vegetable broth, thickening it. Serve and garnish with thinly sliced welsh onions.

KUZU AND DAIKON BLOCKS

1 cup grated daikon
1/2 cup kuzu powder
1 1/4 cups water
1 teaspoon salt
1/2 cup unrefined brown sugar
1/3 cup water
2 tablespoons soy sauce

First dissolve the kuzu powder in a small amount of water. Place the rest of the water in a pot, and then add the kuzu paste to it. Add the grated daikon and salt. Place the pot on medium heat and bring to a boil, then simmer, stirring constantly, for 5 to 6 minutes. Wet the interior of a square mold, about 6 inches long and 1 1/2 inches high, and pour the mixture in. Place in the refrigerator and allow to gel, about 2 hours.

Combine the unrefined brown sugar, 1/3 cup water, and soy sauce in a pan and heat it, simmering for 4 to 5 minutes. Remove the kuzu and daikon block from the mold and cut into serving pieces. Pour the sugar and soy sauce over the blocks and serve.

KUZU AND PICKLED PLUM JELLY

1/2 cup kuzu powder
1 1/4 cups water
4 shredded pickled plums (with pits removed)
3 tablespoons honey

First dissolve the kuzu powder in a small amount of water. Place the rest of the water in a pot, and then add the kuzu paste to it. Place the pot over medium heat and bring to a boil. When the mixture boils, reduce the heat to low and simmer, stirring constantly, for 5 to 6 minutes. Add the shredded pickled plums and honey and blend well. Wet the interior of a square mold, about 6 inches long and 1 1/2 inches high, and pour the mixture in. Place in the refrigerator and allow to gel, about 2 hours. When firm, remove from the mold, cut, and serve.

LOTUS ROOT

For the side effects of aging, heart disease, high blood pressure, stomach ailments, allergies, arteriosclerosis, asthma, coughs, bedwetting, low blood pressure, anemia, diarrhea, headache, kidney ailments, nerve ailments, sinusitis, sleep disorders, colds, nervousness and irritability, problems brought on by menopause, stuffy nose, and hangover. It also promotes healthy skin and physical and sexual vigor and acts as a tonic for the circulatory system.

LOTUS ROOT DUMPLINGS

1 lotus root
$^1/_2$ onion
2 tablespoons kuzu powder
2 tablespoons salt
2 tablespoons vinegar
1 $^1/_3$ tablespoons soy sauce
1 $^1/_3$ tablespoons mirin
$^1/_2$ tablespoon sesame seeds

Grate the unpeeled lotus root. Mince the onion and combine with the grated lotus root. Add the kuzu powder to a small amount of liquid remaining from grating the lotus root and dissolve. Shape the mixture into dumplings about 1 inch in diameter and steam for 15 minutes. Prepare a dressing by mixing together the vinegar, soy sauce, mirin, and sesame seeds and sprinkle it over the dumplings.

LOTUS ROOT
STUFFED
WITH MISO

LOTUS ROOT STUFFED WITH MISO

3 lotus roots about 2 inches in length
$^1/_4$ onion
I tablespoon mirin
2 tablespoons wheat germ
I cup white miso
2 shredded pickled plums (with pits removed)
I tablespoon seaweed flakes
I teaspoon tumeric

Peel the lotus roots and simmer in lightly salted water for 5 minutes, then drain and pat dry. Mince the onion and combine it with the mirin, wheat germ, and white miso. Stir until rather stiff and then divide into three equal portions. Color one portion red by stirring in the shredded pickled plum, a second portion green by stirring in the seaweed flakes, and the third yellow by stirring in the tumeric. Stuff the cavities of each of the three lotus roots with a different color. Slice into $^1/_2$-inch slices and serve.

LOTUS ROOT WITH MISO

$^1/_2$ lotus root
2 tablespoons miso
I tablespoon mirin
I teaspoon grated fresh ginger
minced parsley for garnish
I cup water
I tablespoon vinegar

Cut the unpeeled lotus root into slices I inch thick, then cut the round slices into pie-shaped quarters. Bring the water and vinegar to a boil and add the lotus root. Simmer for 5 minutes. Drain well. Stir together the miso, mirin, and grated ginger, then dress the lotus pieces with the mixture. Garnish with the finely minced parsley.

MILLET

For diabetes and high blood pressure. Rich in the B vitamins, millet warms the body and is an excellent source of physical strength.

MILLET AND VEGETABLE MISO SOUP

^{1}/5 cup millet
3 cups soup stock (page 23)
^{1}/3 cup miso
1 small bunch of spinach or some other green vegetable (mitsuba, snow peas, etc.)
1 inch carrot

Wash the millet and simmer in the soup stock for 10 minutes, until soft. Cut the greens into ^{1}/2-inch lengths. Cut the carrot into matchsticks, and add both the greens and carrot to the millet mixture. Add the miso and stir.

RED AND GREEN MILLET DUMPLINGS

2 cups millet
2^1/2 cups water
2 tablespoons ume shiso
1 teaspoon seaweed flakes
1 teaspoon salt

Wash the millet, place it in a pressure cooker, and seal the lid. Cook over high heat until pressurized, then turn the heat to low and cook for 20 minutes. Remove the pressure cooker from the heat and let it sit with the lid on for 15 to 20 minutes. Remove the lid.

Divide the millet into 2 portions. Mince the ume shiso and stir it into one portion of millet, stirring until the red color spreads evenly.

RED AND GREEN
MILLET DUMPLINGS

MILLET
PORRIDGE

Add the seaweed flakes and salt to the other portion of millet, stirring until the green color spreads evenly. Form the red and green millet into small balls. In Japan, they would be placed on small yakitori sticks and served, but you can also just arrange them in a small bowl.

MILLET PORRIDGE

2/3 cup millet
3 cups water
2 tablespoons salt
sesame salt as needed
4 pickled plums

Wash the millet and simmer it in the water until soft, about 40 minutes. Season with salt, sesame salt, and serve with pickled plums.

MISO

For stomach and liver ailments. It also helps the body expel toxins and impurities.

MISO SOUP

1/2 block tofu
1/3 cup reconstituted wakame
1 deep-fried tofu pocket
4 cups soup stock (page 23)
2/3 cup miso
2 thinly sliced welsh onions

Cut the tofu into 1-inch cubes. Simmer the deep-fried tofu pockets in water for 10 minutes, drain, and wipe away any excess oil. Cut into thin slices. Simmer the tofu and deep-fried tofu strips in the soup stock for about 5 minutes, then add the miso, stir, and simmer an additional minute. Serve in soup bowls and sprinkle with thinly sliced welsh onion.

MISO DIPPING SAUCE

$1/2$ **cup miso**
1 tablespoon mirin
2 tablespoons soup stock (page 23)
2 tablespoons sesame seeds

Combine all ingredients in a pot and simmer for 5 minutes, stirring constantly.

AUTUMN MISO

---

1 burdock
$1/2$ **lotus root**
$1/2$ **small carrot**
$1/2$ **onion**
2 cups soup stock (page 23)
2 cups soybean miso
$1/4$ **cup mirin**
peels of $1/2$ **lemon**
1 fresh ginger root

Mince the unpeeled burdock, lotus root, carrot, and onion. Place the soup stock in a pot and add the minced vegetables. Simmer for 10 minutes until tender, then add the miso and mirin and simmer another 10 minutes, stirring constantly. Mince the ginger root and lemon peels and add to the miso. Stir 2 minutes and serve.

AUTUMN MISO

MOUNTAIN YAM BITS
WITH HONEY-VINEGAR
DRESSING

MOUNTAIN YAM

For digestive ailments, heart disease, low blood pressure, diarrhea, asthma, bedwetting, stomach ailments, weakness, sexual vigor, diabetes, nervousness and irritability, and reproductive organ dysfunctions. It is also a tonic for the circulatory system and promotes milk production in nursing mothers.

GRATED MOUNTAIN YAM SAUCE WITH MISO

4 cups soup stock (page 23)
$2/3$ cup miso
$1/3$ mountain yam
1 teaspoon dried seaweed flakes

Grate the unpeeled yam. Put the soup stock in a pot and bring to a boil. Add the miso and stir. Add the grated mountain yam and bring to a boil one more time. Remove from heat and serve. Garnish with dried seaweed flakes.

MOUNTAIN YAM BITS WITH HONEY-VINEGAR DRESSING

$1/3$ mountain yam
3 tablespoons vinegar
1 tablespoon honey
$1/2$ tablespoon salt
1 sheet of toasted seaweed, crumpled into flakes (page 21)

Cut the unpeeled mountain yam into $3/4$-inch squares. Place them in a clean cloth and pound them lightly until broken into irregular pieces about the size of beans. Then place the mountain yam in a bowl and dress with the vinegar, honey, and salt. Sprinkle the seaweed over the yams.

MOUNTAIN YAM PANCAKES

2/3 mountain yam
1/4 onion, diced
1 tablespoon kuzu powder
3 tablespoons whole wheat flour
1 teaspoon salt
1 tablespoon sesame seeds
3 tablespoons soy sauce
3 tablespoons mirin
2 teaspoons dried seaweed

Grate the unpeeled mountain yam and mix well with the onion, kuzu powder, whole wheat flour, salt, and sesame seeds. Pour the mixture on a baking sheet, forming pancakes about 2 inches in diameter. Bake for 10 minutes at 180 degrees, then remove the pancakes and place on a plate. Combine the soy sauce and mirin to make a sauce, and brush it over the pancakes. Garnish with the seaweed and serve.

**MOUNTAIN YAM
PANCAKES**

GRILLED
FRESH SHIITAKE
WITH SOY SAUCE

MUSHROOMS

For obesity, diabetes, fever, high blood pressure, arteriosclerosis, nerve and liver ailments, colds, and phlegm. They are also anti-carcinogenic and promote healthy skin.

GRILLED FRESH SHIITAKE WITH SOY SAUCE

8 fresh shiitake
2 tablespoons soy sauce
4 thinly sliced welsh onions

Remove the stems from the mushrooms and grill them for about 10 minutes. Use a brush to baste them with soy sauce 2 or 3 times while grilling. Serve on a plate, garnished with the thinly sliced welsh onions.

ENOKI MUSHROOMS WITH SESAME DRESSING

1 pack enoki
1 tablespoon sake
1 teaspoon salt
$1/2$ fresh ginger root
3 tablespoons white sesame seeds
2 teaspoons light soy sauce
2 teaspoons mirin
8 shelled gingko nuts
8 raisins

Cut the enoki into $1/2$-inch lengths and steam for 4 minutes in the sake and salt. Cut the ginger into thin matchsticks. Parch the white sesame seed in a hot pan for 1 minute and then combine with the light soy sauce and mirin and stir into the enoki, coating them well.

Boil the gingko nuts in lightly salted water for 5 minutes. Place the enoki mixture in a dish and garnish with the gingko nuts and raisins.

NATTO

For obesity, liver ailments, sinusitis, stomach ailments, and weakness. It also has anti-carcinogenic properties and is believed to be helpful in preventing harm caused by exposure to radiation. It is an appetite stimulant, promotes sexual vigor, and acts as a tonic for the circulatory system.

NATTO SALAD

1 pack natto
1 teaspoon soy sauce
1 teaspoon Chinese mustard paste
$1/5$ head cabbage
$1/4$ onion
$1/2$ small carrot
4 lettuce leaves
$1/2$ teaspoon parsley
2 tablespoons vinegar
2 tablespoons soy sauce
1 tablespoon ground sesame seeds

Stir the soy sauce and Chinese mustard into the natto. Slice all the vegetables finely and place in an attractive mound. Heap the natto in the middle. Mix the vinegar, soy sauce, and ground sesame together and sprinkle over everything before eating.

NATTO
SALAD

NATTO WITH GARLIC CHIVES

1 bunch garlic chives
1 pack natto
1 1/3 tablespoons soy sauce
1 teaspoon Chinese mustard paste
1/2 tablespoon sesame seeds
1 inch carrot

Parboil the garlic chives for 1 minute, then drain and cut into 1-inch lengths. Combine all the ingredients in a bowl and mix well. Chop the carrot into 1/2-inch cubes and simmer in 1 cup of lightly salted water for 3 minutes. Drain and use them to garnish the natto and garlic chives.

NATTO AND MOUNTAIN YAM WITH PICKLED PLUM

1/3 mountain yam
1 pack natto
3 shredded pickled plums (with pits removed)
1 teaspoon soy sauce
1 welsh onion
1 sheet toasted seaweed, crumpled into flakes (page 21)

Cut the unpeeled mountain yam into 1-inch cubes and mix in with the natto. Put the mountain yam and natto mixture in a bowl and top with the shredded pickled plum, thinly sliced welsh onion, and seaweed flakes.

ONION

For allergies, asthma, chills, colds and flu, diarrhea, hair loss, intestinal parasites, liver ailments, sleep disorders, sore throat, nervousness and irritability, stomach ailments, rashes, diabetes, and colds. Onion also increases stamina and strengthens the circulatory system and the liver and promotes healthy skin and physical stamina.

STEAMED ONIONS WITH VEGETABLES

2 onions
3 reconstituted shiitake mushrooms (page 22)
1 1/2 inches carrot
1 small green pepper
1/3 cup canned corn
1/3 cup reconstituted wakame
2 cups soup stock (page 23)
2 tablespoons mirin
1 tablespoon sake
1 teaspoon salt
1 tablespoon kuzu powder
1 tablespoon water
1 tablespoon grated fresh ginger root

Cut the onions in half across the middle (not lengthwise). Reconstitute the dried shiitake, then cut them, the carrots, and the green pepper into small 1/2-inch squares. Cut the wakame into bite-sized pieces. Score the bottoms of the onion halves lightly and steam them in about 1/2 inch of water for about 10 minutes in a heavy skillet over medium heat. Add the soup stock and the chopped vegetables

STEAMED ONIONS
WITH VEGETABLES

to another pot and simmer for about 1 minute. When the vegetables are tender, add the mirin, sake, and salt. Drop a few drops of water into the kuzu powder to form a paste, and then slowly add it to the pot of vegetables and stock as a thickener. Place the onion halves on serving dishes and pour the vegetable sauce over them. Garnish with grated ginger root.

ONION WITH SESAME DRESSING

1 onion
1 tablespoon soy sauce
1 tablespoon mirin
3 tablespoons white sesame seeds
minced parboiled green vegetables for garnish

Slice the onion thinly and boil it in lightly salted water for about 1 minute. Parch the sesame seeds for about 1 minute in a heavy pan and then grind them in a mortar. Toss together the onion, soy sauce, mirin, and ground sesame seeds, serve, and garnish with a touch of green—minced parboiled snow peas, spinach, or broccoli.

PICKLED PLUM

For tiredness, the side effects of aging, allergies, anemia, asthma, poor appetite, digestive ailments, stomach ailments, constipation, diarrhea, hemorrhoids, intestinal parasites, liver ailments, low blood pressure, symptoms of menopause, nerve ailments, sinusitis, sore throat, motion sickness, and mental or emotional stress. Especially effective for colds and flu. The pickled plum can be eaten whole, or you can remove the pit, dice the meat, and press the juice out of it and drink it. Pressing the pickled plum meat to the temples relieves headache. Pickled plum also has anti-carcinogenic properties and is a tonic for the circulatory system.

PICKLED PLUM BANCHA

4 pickled plums
1 teaspoon ginger juice
2 teaspoons soy sauce
3 cups bancha (roasted Japanese tea)

An excellent natural cold remedy, this recipe makes 4 cups of tea.
Place each pickled plum in tea cup. Add ginger juice and soy sauce,
then pour in the hot bancha. You can substitute black tea, Oolong
tea, or Japanese green tea for the bancha.

PICKLED PLUMS TOSSED WITH ONION

1 onion
3 shredded pickled plums (with pits removed)
1 tablespoon mirin
minced parsley for garnish

Slice the onion thinly and parboil for 30 seconds. Drain and pat dry
and mix with the shredded pickled plum and mirin. Serve and garnish
with parsley.

PICKLED PLUM AND WAKAME SOUP

4 pickled plums
1 cup reconstituted wakame
4 cups soup stock (page 23)
2 thinly sliced welsh onions
salt and pepper for seasoning

Place the soup stock in a pot and add the wakame. Simmer for 3
minutes. Season with salt and pepper. Place the pickled plums in a

**PICKLED PLUMS
TOSSED WITH
ONION**

(clockwise from bottom left)
**OVERNIGHT PICKLES:
DAIKON, MUSTARD GREENS,
AND CHINESE CABBAGE**

**BRAN PICKLES:
BAMBOOSHOOTS,
CUCUMBERS,
AND CARROTS**

dish and pour the broth over them. Garnish with the thinly sliced welsh onion.

PICKLES

For poor appetite, stomach ailments, and constipation.

OVERNIGHT PICKLES

^{1}/4 head cabbage
1 small carrot
1 onion
3 tablespoons salt
2 tablespoons sake

Chop all the vegetables into matchsticks and stir them together in a large bowl. Sprinkle them with salt and sake. Place a lid over the vegetables and weight it down with a heavy stone or four or five dishes. Allow the vegetables to pickle overnight. Before eating drain any excess liquid. Serve sprinkled with sesame seeds or chopped or grated nuts.

You can make delicious pickles using this recipe with many other vegetables, including cucumbers, daikon, Chinese cabbage, or romaine or bib lettuce.

RICE BRAN PICKLES

4^1/2 pounds (25–30 cups) rice bran
1^1/2 cups salt
3 red chili peppers, cut in 2 or 3
3 tablespoons Chinese mustard
5 cups or more water that has been boiled and then allowed to cool

Place the rice bran in a large pot or cauldron over low heat, stirring vigorously for 6 to 7 minutes to disinfect the bran and also bring out its aroma. Place all the ingredients in a large earthen pot or plastic bucket and stir well until the mixture has the consistency of a thick paste. Combine a few cups of leftover vegetables—cabbage, carrots, cucumbers, or whatever is available—for a starter and add to the rice bran mixture. Cover with a clean cloth and keep in a cool place. Stir the mixture well at least once a day, twice or three times is better. After about a week the rice bran mixture will "mature." At this point you can remove the starter vegetables and discard them, or you can eat them, chopping them finely and sprinkling with seasame seed.

You can pickle cucumbers, daikon slices, carrots, cabbage, okra, turnips, turnip or daikon greens, watermelon rinds, or any other seasonal vegetable. Sprinkle them lightly with salt and squeeze out any excess water before burying them in the rice bran. Leave them in the bran for 5 to 6 hours in the summer, or 12 hours in the winter.

PUMPKIN

For colds, diabetes, asthma, kidney ailments, liver ailments, sleep disorders, weakness, anemia, prostate problems. It also promotes healthy skin, healthy growth in young children, and it helps the body rid itself of impurities and poisons.

PUMPKIN BALLS

¹/₄ of a small Japanese pumpkin
2 tablespoons dried raisins
2 inches carrot
I teaspoon salt

Cut the quarter of an unpeeled pumpkin into slices about I inch thick, so that they will cook faster, and steam for 15 minutes. While still warm, place in a mortar or bowl and mash. Add the salt and mix

PUMPKIN
BALLS

PUMPKIN
POTAGE

well. Take a clean, white, slightly damp rag and place a small amount—enough to form a ball about 1 inch in diameter—of pumpkin in the center of the cloth. Form the pumpkin into a ball and then give the top of the cloth a twist. It will leave marks on the pumpkin ball as shown in the photograph. This recipe should make 8 to 10 pumpkin balls. Place the balls in a serving dish and garnish with the raisins.

PUMPKIN POTAGE

1/3 **pumpkin**
1 **onion**
1 **cup cooked brown rice**
4 **cups soup stock (page 23)**
1 1/3 **tablespoons salt**
dash of pepper
roasted pumpkin seeds and minced parsley for garnish

Cut the pumpkin and onion into slices about 1 inch thick. Place 3 cups of the soup stock in a pot, add the vegetables, and simmer for 10 minutes until they are soft. Add the cooked brown rice, then pour the entire mixture in a blender and blend for 1 minute. Return the blended mixture to the stove and add the remaining 1 cup of soup stock. Season with salt and pepper. Serve in soup bowls and garnish with roasted pumpkin seeds and parsley.

¹/5 small Japanese pumpkin
¹/2 onion
¹/2 cup boiled azuki beans (page 16)
4 cups soup stock (page 23)
²/3 cup miso

Cut the unpeeled pumpkin and the onion into ¹/2-inch cubes. Place the soup stock in a pot and add the pumpkin. Simmer for 10 minutes, until the pumpkin is tender. Drain the azuki beans and add to the pumpkin mixture. Stir in the miso until dissolved and bring to a boil. Remove from heat and serve.

SEA VEGETABLES

For allergies, asthma, retarded growth and development, nervousness and irritability, constipation, nerve ailments, sinusitis, obesity, diabetes, arteriosclerosis, heart disease, reproductive organ dysfunctions, hemorrhoids, kidney ailments, liver ailments, sore throat, high blood pressure, anemia, and goiter. They also promote sexual vigor, healthy skin, prevent graying hair, and act as a tonic for the circulatory system.

**POLKA-DOT
SOUP**

HIJIKI AND
LOTUS ROOT

HIJIKI AND LOTUS ROOT

1 cup hijiki, reconstituted (page 21)
1/2 lotus root
1 cup soup stock (page 23)
4 tablespoons soy sauce
2 tablespoons mirin
2 tablespoons sake
1 1/2 tablespoons ground white sesame seeds

Cut the lotus root into rounds 1 1/2 inches thick. Place the lotus root slices and hijiki in a pot and add the soup stock. Place the pan over medium heat and simmer for 10 minutes. When the vegetables are tender, add the soy sauce, mirin, and sake and simmer another 3 to 4 minutes. Garnish with the sesame seeds.

KOMBU SIMMERED WITH VEGETABLES

4 inches kombu
2 shiitake mushrooms, reconstituted (page 21)
1/2 burdock
1/2 small carrot
1/4 lotus root
2 cups soup stock (page 23)
2 tablespoons soy sauce
1 1/2 tablespoons mirin
1 1/2 tablespoons sake

Cut all the vegetables into 1-inch lengths and place them in a pot with the soup stock. Simmer for 5 to 6 minutes. Add the soy sauce, mirin, and sake and simmer for another 5 minutes.

WAKAME IN SESAME VINEGAR DRESSING

1 cup reconstituted wakame
10 snow peas
3 tablespoons white sesame seeds
1 tablespoon vinegar
$^1/_2$ teaspoon salt
1 tablespoon light soy sauce

Cut the wakame into 1-inch square pieces. Parboil the snow peas for about 1 minute in lightly salted water, then cut them into slices at an angle. Mix the wakame, snow peas, and white sesame seeds and dress with the vinegar, salt, and light soy sauce.

SESAME

For chronic stomach ailments, nerve inflammation, allergies, headache, heart disease, hemorrhoids, liver ailments, nerve ailments, sinusitis, weakness, high blood pressure, constipation, kidney ailments, night blindness, hemorrhoids, anemia, lack of milk production, frequent urination during the night, and graying hair. It also promotes sexual vigor and healthy skin.

SESAME DRESSING OVER CARROTS

1 small carrot
1 tablespoon soy sauce
1 tablespoon mirin
2 tablespoons ground white sesame seeds

Cut the carrot into matchstick slices and simmer for 2 minutes in lightly salted water. Drain, rinse, and shake out any excess water. Mix the soy sauce, mirin, and sesame seeds and dress the carrots with the mixture before serving.

SESAME SYRUP

3 cups water
$^1/_4$ cup sesame paste (page 22)
1 tablespoon kuzu powder
1$^1/_2$ tablespoons honey
pine nuts as needed

Combine all the ingredients except the pine nuts in a pan and simmer, stirring constantly, for 2 minutes. Serve and garnish with pine nuts.

SESAME SALT

10 tablespoons black sesame seeds
1 tablespoon sea salt

In a heavy frying pan saute the salt, being careful not to burn it, for about 3 minutes. Place it in a mortar and grind fine. Heat up the pan again and saute the sesame seed, half at a time, for about 1 minute over medium heat, until they are fragrant. Add the sesame seeds to the mortar and grind lightly for about 5 minutes. After the mixture has cooled, place it in a jar. It should be used within 4 or 5 days.

SESAME TOFU

7 cups soup stock (page 23)
I cup kuzu powder
$^1/_2$ cup sesame paste
I tablespoon mirin
I tablespoon sake
grated ginger and soy sauce as needed

This dish is molded to resemble a rectangular block of tofu, but you can use molds of other shapes if you like.

Place the soup stock in a pan and dissolve the kuzu powder in it. Add the sesame paste, sake, and mirin, and heat, stirring regularly until the mixture boils. After bringing it to a boil, cook over low heat for about 20 minutes.

Wet the inside of a square mold and pour in the mixture. Float the mold in a pan of cool water until the mixture is cool, then refrigerate for I hour, until it gels. Remove it from the mold and cut it into serving sizes. Sprinkle a little grated ginger and soy sauce on each serving.

SESAME
TOFU

SOY SAUCE

Soy sauce stimulates the metabolism.

SOY SAUCE AND VINEGAR DRESSING

4 tablespoons vinegar
3 tablespoons soy sauce
2/3 tablespoon mirin

Mix well together and use as a dressing over seaweed and fresh or cooked vegetables.

SWEET SOY SAUCE AND VINEGAR DRESSING

4 tablespoons vinegar
3 tablespoons soy sauce
I tablespoon honey

Mix well together and use as a marinade for daikon or turnip, or a dressing over seaweed and fresh or cooked vegetables.

DILUTED SOY SAUCE

2 tablespoons soy sauce
2 tablespoons soup stock (page 23)

Mix well together and use as a dressing over chilled or boiled tofu.

SOYBEANS

For stomach ailments, constipation, diabetes, heart disease, colds and flu, hemorrhoids, weakness, liver ailments, nerve ailments, arteriosclerosis, and the side effects of the aging process. They also promote milk production in nursing mothers, act as a tonic for the circulatory system, and promote healthy skin.

SOYBEAN POTAGE

$^1/_5$ cup dried soybeans
4 cups soup stock (page 23)
2 inches daikon
$^1/_4$ medium carrot
3 taro tubers
2 finely sliced welsh onions
$^2/_3$ cup miso

Wash the beans and soak them in 1 cup of water for 8 hours. Cut the daikon, carrot, and taro into $^1/_4$-inch slices and simmer them in the soup stock until tender. Place the beans, now swollen and tender, together with any remaining liquid and an additional 1 cup of water in a blender or food processor. Blend for 2 minutes. Add the miso to the vegetables and stock and stir it in. Then add the blended beans and thinly sliced welsh onion to the vegetables and miso and reheat before serving.

SOYBEANS
WITH MIXED
VEGETABLES

SOYBEAN SPROUT SALAD

1 cup sprouted soybeans (page 23)
1/5 head cabbage
1/3 medium carrot
4 tablespoons vinegar
2 teaspoons salt
dash of pepper
minced parsley for a garnish

Simmer the sprouted beans in lightly salted water for about 10
minutes. As an alternative, you can steam the sprouts. Chop the
cabbage and carrots into thin matchsticks. Place them in a bowl and
sprinkle the bean sprouts over them. Mix together a dressing of
the vinegar, salt, and pepper and sprinkle it over the salad. Garnish
with minced parsley.

SOYBEANS WITH MIXED VEGETABLES

1 cup dried soybeans
1/2 burdock root
1/2 lotus root
1/2 medium carrot
1/2 cube konnyaku
3 dried shiitake mushrooms
minced parsley as needed
3 cups soup stock (page 23)
1/3 cup light soy sauce
2 tablespoons sake
3 tablespoons mirin

Wash the soybeans and place them in a pressure cooker with 3 cups
of water, and soak for 8 hours. Cook over high heat until pressurized, turn the heat to low and cook 3 minutes. Remove from heat
and allow to cool.

Cut the vegetables into cubes about 1/2 inch square, then combine with the beans and add the soup stock. Simmer for 10 minutes, then season with the soy sauce, sake, and mirin. Serve in a bowl and sprinkle with parsley.

SPINACH

For anemia, bedwetting, chills, nervous disorders, menopausal symptoms, constipation, diabetes, heart disease, kidney ailments, liver ailments, low blood pressure, and stomach ailments. It also promotes strength, healthy skin, and acts as a tonic for the circulatory system.

SPINACH ROLLS

1 bunch spinach
2 rectangular or triangular deep-fried tofu pockets
1 cup soup stock (page 23)
1 tablespoon light soy sauce

Parboil the spinach in water with about 1 teaspoon salt for 1 minute. Immediately rinse with cold water and press out all excess water. Sprinkle with the light soy sauce. Simmer the deep-fried tofu pockets in water for 10 minutes, then drain and wipe off any oil. Simmer for another 5 minutes in the soup stock and light soy sauce. Slit open the deep-fried tofu pocket and open it up to a square, exposing the inside. Place half the spinach at the bottom edge of each pocket and roll them up. Then cut each pocket into eight equal lengths and serve.

SPINACH
ROLLS

SPINACH WITH CREAM SAUCE

1 bunch spinach
1 inch carrot
$1/2$ cup tofu milk
2 tablespoons kuzu powder
$1/2$ tablespoon salt
pepper as needed

Parboil the spinach for 1 minute, then drain and cut into 1 1/4-inch lengths. Squeeze all excess water out of the spinach. Slice the carrots into thin matchsticks and boil in lightly salted water for 1 minute. Place the tofu milk, kuzu powder, salt, and pepper in a pot and simmer for 2 minutes, stirring constantly, until the mixture thickens. Add the spinach and carrots to the sauce, stir, and serve.

SPINACH WITH SESAME DRESSING

1 1/2 bunches spinach
2 tablespoons soy sauce
1 tablespoon mirin
1 tablespoon sake
1 tablespoon white sesame seeds

Parboil the spinach in salted water for 1 minute. Immediately rinse with cold water and press out all excess water. Cut into 1-inch lengths. Grind the white sesame seeds in a mortar and then add the soy sauce, mirin, and sake. Continue stirring until smooth, then dress the spinach with the mixture and serve.

TARO

For constipation, fever, asthma, toothache, and nerve ailments.

TARO TORTOISE SHELLS

8 taro tubers
2 cups soup stock (page 23)
2¹/₂ tablespoons soy sauce
I tablespoon mirin
I tablespoon sake
¹/₃ chili pepper
a few minced lemon skin shavings for garnish

Peel the taro tubers and trim them into a hexagonal shape, like a tortoise shell. Place the soup stock in a pot, add the taro "tortoise shells," and simmer for 15 minutes until the taro is soft. Add the soy sauce, mirin, sake, and chili pepper and simmer another 6 minutes. Serve and garnish with the minced lemon skin.

FLUFFY MASHED TARO
WITH APPLES, RAISINS,
AND CINNAMON

FLUFFY MASHED TARO WITH APPLES, RAISINS, AND CINNAMON

6 taro tubers
2 tablespoons honey
1 teaspoon salt
1/2 apple
2 tablespoons raisins
1/2 teaspoon cinnamon

Steam the taro with the skin on for 30 minutes, then peel. Place the peeled taro, while still warm, in a mortar and mash. Add the honey and salt and mix well. Core the apple and slice it into 8 wedges. Further slice the wedges into thin slices. Soak for 1 minute in lightly salted water and then drain and pat dry. Combine the mashed taro and the apple slices and toss gently. Serve and sprinkle with cinnamon.

TARO STEW WITH DUMPLINGS

1 cup soba flour
1/2 cup brown rice flour
1/2 cup whole wheat flour
1 teaspoon salt
1 1/2 cups water
6 cups soup stock (page 23)
5 taro tubers
1 small carrot
3 fresh shiitake mushrooms
1/2 pack shimeji mushrooms
1/5 lotus root
1/4 block konnyaku (can be omitted if not available)
2 finely sliced welsh onions
1 cup miso

Peel the taro and cut it into 1-inch cubes. Cut the unpeeled carrot and lotus root into slices 1/4-inch thick and then cut the slices into

TARO STEW
WITH DUMPLINGS

pie-shaped quarters. Cut the shiitake in half. Break up the shimeji clumps into smaller clumps of 3 or 4 mushrooms. Cut the konnyaku into 1-inch cubes. Combine all of these ingredients with the soup stock and simmer for 5 minutes. To make dumplings, combine the 3 types of flour with the salt and water and stir vigorously for 5 minutes. Then drop the dough into the simmering soup a tablespoon at a time. When the dumplings all float to the top of the stock, stir in the miso and then turn off the heat. Serve and garnish with the thinly sliced welsh onion.

TOFU

For stomach ailments, diabetes, aging, arteriosclerosis, heart disease, obesity, allergies, nerve ailments, sore throat, high blood pressure, and liver ailments. It also promotes healthy skin.

TOFU GRILLED IN MISO

1 1/2 blocks tofu
1/2 cup white miso
2 tablespoons sesame paste (page 22)
1 1/3 tablespoons mirin
1/2 cup red miso
2 tablespoons sesame paste (page 22)
1 1/3 tablespoons mirin
shaved lemon peel and seaweed flakes for garnish

Cut the tofu into 8 equal-sized pieces and place them on a baking pan. Prepare the white miso mixture by stirring together the white miso, sesame paste, and mirin, and the red miso mixture in the same way. Coat half with the white miso mixture and half with the red miso mixture. Bake at 480 degrees for 10 minutes. Move to a serving plate and garnish with shaved lemon peel and seaweed flakes.

TOFU
CHEESE

TOFU CHEESE

¹/₂ block tofu
6 tablespoons sesame paste (page 22)
2 tablespoons white miso
2 teaspoons salt
2 tablespoons vinegar
pepper as needed

Cut each tofu block into 4 and simmer in water for 4 to 5 minutes. Drain and shake out excess water. Place the tofu in a blender with the rest of the ingredients and blend for 30 seconds. Eat as is, or spread on bread or crackers.

TOFU IN BROTH

1 ¹/₂ blocks tofu
4 cups water
4 inches kombu for stock
¹/₃ cup soy sauce
¹/₂ grated fresh ginger root
2 tablespoons ground sesame seeds
2 thinly sliced welsh onions

Place the water and kombu in a heavy pot. Since this dish is eaten out of the pot, a decorative earthenware pot such as used for preparing sukiyaki or shabu-shabu is ideal. Cut the tofu into 8 equal pieces and simmer for 4 to 5 minutes. Spoon the tofu cubes out of the pot and place on a small serving dish as you eat. Season by sprinkling with the soy sauce, grated ginger, ground sesame seeds, and thinly sliced welsh onions.

CHILLED TOFU

2 blocks of tofu
$^1/_2$ small carrot
4 shiitake mushrooms
$^1/_2$ cup soup stock (page 23)
2 teaspoons mirin
2 teaspoons soy sauce
small amount of any finely diced green vegetable, as a topping
2 minced pickled plums (with pits removed)
$^1/_2$ grated fresh ginger root
2 tablespoons soy sauce

Slice the carrots into matchsticks and parboil them and the green vegetable—snow peas, spinach, or broccoli—in slightly salted water for 1 minute. Slice the reconstituted shiitake into matchsticks and simmer in the soup stock, mirin, and 2 teaspoons soy sauce for 5 minutes. Drain. Cut the tofu blocks in half and top them with the carrots, greens, shiitake, shredded plum, and grated ginger. Sprinkle soy sauce on them just before eating.

CHILLED
TOFU

The "weathermark" identifies this book as a production of Weatherhill, Inc., publishers of fine books on Asia and the Pacific. Editorial supervision: Jeffrey Hunter. Book and cover design: Liz Trovato. Production supervision: Bill Rose. Printed and bound by Oceanic Graphic Printing, Hong Kong. The typeface used is Gill Sans.